Germany

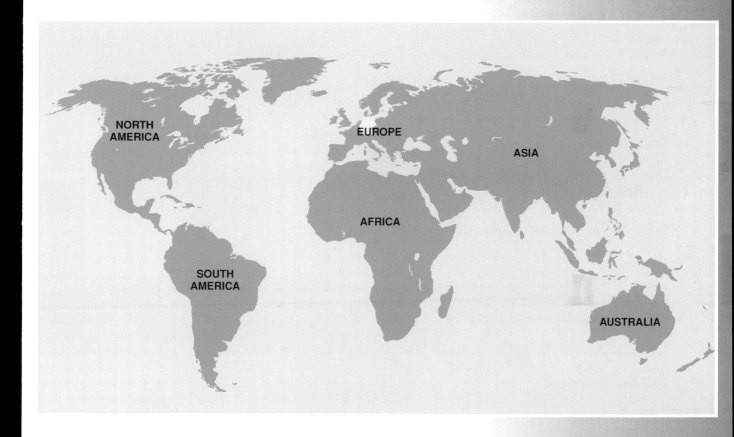

NORTH
AMERICA

EUROPE

ASIA

AFRICA

SOUTH
AMERICA

AUSTRALIA

Clare Boast

Heinemann
L I B R A R Y

First published in Great Britain by Heinemann Library
Halley Court, Jordan Hill, Oxford OX2 8EJ
a division of Reed Educational and Professional Publishing Ltd

OXFORD FLORENCE PRAGUE MADRID ATHENS
MELBOURNE AUCKLAND KUALA LUMPUR SINGAPORE TOKYO
IBADAN NAIROBI KAMPALA JOHANNESBURG GABORONE
PORTSMOUTH NH CHICAGO MEXICO CITY SAO PAULO

Designed by AMR
Illustrations by Art Construction
Printed and bound in Italy by L.E.G.O.

01 00 99 98 97
10 9 8 7 6 5 4 3 2 1

ISBN 0 431 04538 0

British Library Cataloguing in Publication Data

Boast, Clare
Step into Germany
1. Germany – Geography – Juvenile literature
I. Title II. Germany
914.3

Acknowledgements
The Publishers would like to thank the following for permission to reproduce photographs:
J. Allan Cash pp.7, 8; Art Directors p.4; Trevor Clifford pp.10, 12–13, 16–17, 25; Colorific!
Reinhard Janke/focus p.27, Alon Reininger/Contact p.18, Peter Turnley/Black Star p.28, Michael
Yamashita p.24; Robert Harding Picture Library p.11; Katz Pictures Nascimento/Rea p.15, Tom
Stoddart p.5; Spectrum Colour Library p.29; Trip David Cumming pp.14, 19, 22, Eric Smith p.26,
R Styles p.6; A Tovy p.9, Trip p.23.

Cover photograph reproduced with permission of:
   background: Tony Stone Images, Stephen Studd
   child: Image Bank.

Our thanks to Betty Root for her comments in the preparation of this book.

Every effort has been made to contact copyright holders of any material reproduced in this
book. Any omissions will be rectified in subsequent printings if notice is given to the Publisher.

CONTENTS

INTRODUCTION

There are many old castles in Bavaria, an area in the south of Germany.

WHERE IS GERMANY?

Germany is in the middle of Europe. It has borders with nine other countries. It has coastlines on the North Sea and the Baltic Sea.

GERMANY'S HISTORY

Germany was part of the **Roman Empire** for about 500 years. After that, it divided into many smaller countries but became one country again.

After the Second World War, in 1949, Germany was divided into two: East Germany and West Germany. Even the capital city, Berlin, was split into two. A wall was built across the city where it was divided.

Pieces of the Berlin Wall are being sold as souvenirs. Many tourists want a piece of the wall that split Berlin.

Lots of ordinary people took part in pulling down the Berlin Wall in 1989.

People in East and West Germany led different lives. People were better off in West Germany than in East Germany. The wall was knocked down in 1989. In 1990 East and West Germany became one country. But it will take some time before everyone has the same chance of a good way of life.

THE LAND

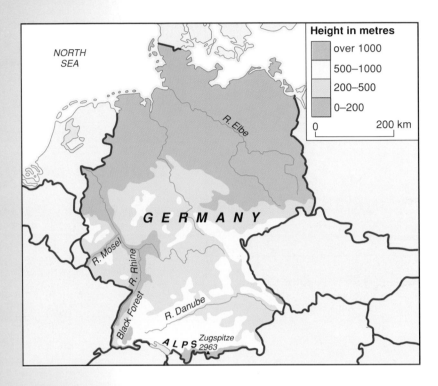

Height in metres

- over 1000
- 500–1000
- 200–500
- 0–200

0   200 km

NORTH SEA

R. Elbe

GERMANY

R. Mosel

R. Rhine

Black Forest

R. Danube

ALPS   Zugspitze 2963

PLAINS

The north of Germany is a large **plain**. It has some low hills and valleys made by rivers that run to the North Sea. The soil is very good for farming.

The River Moselle has carved out a steep-sided valley here.

6

The plains are very flat in places. Farmers can use big farm machines to cut the wheat.

PLATEAU LAND

The middle of Germany has areas of **plateau** land, broken up by mountains. Some of these mountains are made from the **lava** of old **volcanoes**.

MOUNTAINS

The south of Germany has lots of mountains. The highest mountains are in the far south. They are the Alps. They separate Germany from other countries.

The highest place in Germany is on top of Zugspitze mountain in the Alps. It is almost 3000 m high.

7

WEATHER, PLANTS AND ANIMALS

In summer Berlin is sunny and warm. But in winter, temperatures can be well below freezing.

THE WEATHER

All over Germany people have to be prepared for warm summers and cold winters, especially when the wind blows from the north and east.

Different parts of Germany have different weather. The mountains in the south are always colder and wetter than the low flat plains in the north.

PLANTS AND ANIMALS

Nearly a third of Germany is covered in forests. High in the mountains there are fir trees. Further down, oak and maple trees grow. Most flat land has been cleared for farming or factories. But there are heaths where the soil is not rich enough for things to grow.

Some mountain areas have been made **national parks**. Wild boar and deer live there. Foxes and badgers live all over Germany.

Germany has a lot of forests, but many of the trees are being killed by acid rain. This is rain polluted by the smoke from factories.

The Black Forest gets its name from the dark fir trees that grow there.

TOWNS AND CITIES

There has been a town at this place on the River Danube for more than 2000 years.

Lots of German towns have old centres. These towns have grown steadily as new houses, factories and offices are built.

BERLIN

Before 1990, Bonn was the capital city of West Germany and East Berlin was the capital of East Germany. Berlin will be the capital of the United Germany in the year 2000. Until then, the country will be run from both cities.

TOURISM AND INDUSTRY

Different German towns have grown for different reasons. The area known as the Ruhr has lots of towns. They are almost joined together with many mines and factories. Other towns are busy ports, like Hamburg. Then there are the **tourist** towns, like the old town of Nuremberg.

There is a toy fair in Nuremberg each year. People from all over the world come to it.

Nuremberg town centre has a special Christmas market. Crowds of people come from all around.

LIVING IN STUTTGART

THE BERGER FAMILY

Markus and Heike Berger live in a flat on the edge of the city of Stuttgart. They have six-year-old twin girls, Ruth and Hannah, and a boy, Jonathan (who is one).

THE FAMILY'S DAY

Markus runs a nearby factory. Heike runs the house and looks after the children.

The twins go to a local school all day, but they come home for lunch.

The family live on the top floor of a block of flats.

Heike cycles to lots of places with Jonathan.

These shops are near the family's flat.

The family eat their evening meal together. They are eating spaghetti bolognese.

Markus's factory is close enough for him to cycle to work.

MEALTIMES

The family eat together most evenings. They like all sorts of different food. Heike has plenty of time to shop and cook, although she needs to be home to make lunch for the twins.

TIME OFF

The family like to go for bicycle rides. They are close to the country, because they live in a **suburb**, on the edge of Stuttgart.

Heike takes the car to the supermarket to get a lot of food in one go.

13

FARMING IN GERMANY

Germany is a rich country because of its industry. Not many people work in farming. About 70% of German farms are too small to make a profit. Farming will only make money if the small farms join up to make larger ones.

SPECIAL CROPS

Some farmers grow just one crop. Two such crops are used to make drinks – grapes make wine and hops make beer.

Grapes are grown in vineyards. Grapes can grow in places that are too steep for other crops. But they need warm, sunny weather.

OTHER FARMS

Many smaller farms grow crops and keep animals too. They keep cows, sheep, pigs and chickens. They grow fruit like plums, apples and pears.

FARMS IN THE NORTH

The best land for farming is on the flat **plains** in the north of Germany. The weather and soil are good for farming. The farms there are the biggest and most profitable. They mainly grow wheat, barley, oats and potatoes.

Potato harvesters on a farm in the east of Germany.

Before Germany became one country the farms in East Germany were run by the government. Now people run their own farms.

LIVING IN THE COUNTRY

THE GAISBAUER FAMILY

Hans and Gisela Gaisbauer live in a house on the edge of the town of Passau, in the south of Germany. Passau is near a big forest.

Hans and Gisela have two girls, Ute, (who is thirteen) and Almut (eight). They have one boy, Felix (eleven).

Hans at work in the forest, looking after the trees.

Ute is learning to play the recorder.

Gisela does most of her shopping in a weekly trip to Passau.

The family are eating their evening meal of fried meat in breadcrumbs, mashed potatoes and salad.

The children have a big garden where they keep their rabbits.

THE FAMILY'S DAY

Hans is a forest ranger. He works in the nearby forest, clearing away old and fallen trees, looking after young trees and planting new ones.

Gisela works part-time at a local school. The children go to school. German schools run from 8 am to 1 pm. There is always homework.

MEALTIMES

The family eat breakfast together in the morning. They eat their main meal in the evening. They eat bread, meat and vegetables. A favourite meal is meat loaf and potato dumplings.

Felix and Almut go to their school by bus. Ute can walk to hers.

GERMAN SHOPS

A shopping arcade in Hamburg. Many towns and cities have covered shopping arcades.

BIG SHOPS

Germany is a rich country with lots of shops. There are fewer small shops selling one thing, than big shops selling lots of things. Even people who live near little shops prefer to drive to a supermarket for their shopping.

Hypermarkets (huge supermarkets) are on the edges of towns, with lots of parking space for cars.

Cars and buses are not allowed to drive through this pedestrian precinct in Cologne.

SPECIAL SHOPS

Some small shops have managed to stay open by selling special things. Some shops sell just cheese, with special cheeses that supermarkets do not sell.

PEDESTRIAN PRECINCTS

Many cities have pedestrian precincts where cars and buses are not allowed. People can walk around the shops and there is more space for outdoor cafés and small stalls. It is safer and there is less **pollution**, too.

German shops do not use throw-away plastic carrier bags. Many shops also have places set up to recycle packaging.

GERMAN FOOD

TRADITIONAL FOOD

Different parts of Germany have different traditional foods. These foods are usually found locally. So areas near the sea have lots of fish recipes – like the fish soup from Hamburg. There are lots of different sausages. Frankfurters are a sausage that used to be made just in Frankfurt. Now they are eaten in hot dogs all over the world.

People make traditional food with local fish, meat and vegetables like these.

Bread is eaten with almost every meal. There are about 300 different types of bread.

MEAT AND VEGETABLES

Germans eat more meat, on average, than people in most other countries. German sausages are famous. You can buy them to cook. You can also buy them already cooked and spiced, like salami.

People do not eat just meat. Potatoes and green vegetables are eaten almost every day. Cabbage is eaten fresh or pickled with vinegar and spices.

German breads are made with many different sorts of flour. Some bread is flavoured or topped with seeds.

21

MADE IN GERMANY

Germany is a very industrialized country. This means it has a lot of factories that make things. German factories make iron, steel and chemicals or **goods** – like cars, washing machines, microwave cookers and CD players.

This mine in the west of Germany is mining brown coal. The coal is burned to make electricity.

Germany sells a lot of these goods to other countries. Goods sold to other countries are called **exports**.

These robots are making **BMW** cars. German factories use the newest ideas and ways of working.

POLLUTION

Pollution is a big problem in Germany. This is partly because there are so many factories. It is also because some factories, especially in what was East Germany, were not built to avoid making pollution. But people realize there is a problem and are trying to modernize the factories and clean up the pollution.

Germany digs up more brown coal than any other country in the world.

23

GETTING AROUND

Germany has a very good system of roads, railways and waterways for getting around the country. Most of the big cities have airports, too.

ROADS

German autobahns were the first ever motorways. The first one was built about 50 years ago, and they have been added to ever since. There is no speed limit on these motorways – people can drive as fast as they like.

An autobahn near Berlin. Most people and goods are moved around the country by road.

Trams in Stuttgart run on rails on the road. They have their own routes and stops, just like buses.

TRAINS AND BOATS

All the big cities are linked by high speed trains. The fastest of these travels at about 280 kilometres per hour. You can get to smaller places on slower trains.

There are a lot of rivers and **canals** in Germany that are used to move **goods** and people around. They link towns and cities with the sea.

Most cities have good bus and tram services. Big cities like Berlin and Munich have their own underground railways.

SPORTS AND HOLIDAYS

SPORTS

Many people in Germany enjoy watching and playing sport, especially football, tennis, athletics, sailing and skiing. Some people enjoy newer sports like hang-gliding or sailboarding.

PARKS

Germany has lots of parks with adventure trails and sports fields. There are playgrounds for the children, too. Some parks are built on land where factories used to be.

A hang-glider's view of Bavaria. Mountain air currents are good for hang-gliding.

TIME OFF

Some people who live in the cities like to get to the country at the weekend. Some of them prefer to stay in the city, visiting the shops, museums, bars and cafés.

HOLIDAYS

Many Germans go to another country on holiday. But they also go to different parts of Germany. They might go skiing in the mountains, or camping in the forests. They also like to go to the beaches on the **coast**.

Germany's football team has won the World Cup three times.

Football fans at a cup final match in Berlin.

FESTIVALS AND ARTS

The Munich Beer Festival celebrates harvest time.

FESTIVALS

Some German festivals, like Christmas and Easter, are religious. Germany began the tradition of Christmas trees.

Germany has lots of festivals that are not religious. Some of them celebrate harvest time. The Octoberfest (October Feast) in Munich is a big festival. It is also called the Beer Festival (hops and barley for beer are important local crops). People come to it from all over the world.

ARTS

Many German music composers are famous all over Europe. Bach, Beethoven and Wagner were all German composers. German orchestras and choirs perform all over the world. German artists are famous, too. Holbein (who lived in the 1500s) went to England to paint royalty and rich people.

Most of the fairy-tales that we are told as children, like *Hansel and Gretel* or *Rumpelstiltskin*, were written by the Grimm brothers, who were German.

This is the Children's Festival in the town of Dinkelsbürg. People dress in traditional clothes and dance in the street.

Decorating Christmas trees with lights is a custom that comes from Germany.

GERMANY FACTFILE

People

People from Germany are called Germans.

Capital city

From 2000, the capital city of Germany will be Berlin.

Largest cities

Berlin is the largest city in Germany with nearly three million people. The second largest city is Hamburg and Munich is the third largest city.

Head of country

Germany is ruled by a president and a **government**. The head of the government is called the chancellor.

Population

There are 82 million people living in Germany.

Money

The money in Germany is called the Deutschmark.

Language

People in Germany speak German.

Religion

Most people in Germany are either Protestant or Roman Catholic.

GLOSSARY

canal a river that has been made by people

exports things that are sold to other countries

goods things that people have made

government people who run the country. In Germany the government is chosen by the people.

lava melted rock from a volcano

national park an area of land set aside by the government to protect the animals and plants there

plains a large area of flat land

plateau a high, flat area of land

pollution dirty air, water or land

Roman Empire the Romans were people who, starting from Rome in Italy, took over much of Europe and other parts of the world from about 750BC to AD300

souvenir a thing that reminds someone of a place they have been to

suburbs the edges of cities where people live

tourist somebody who visits a place on holiday

volcano a mountain that sometimes erupts

INDEX

BUGS BUNNY
Too Many Carrots

by Jean Lewis

illustrated by Peter Alvarado and Bob Totten

GOLDEN PRESS
Western Publishing Company, Inc.
Racine, Wisconsin

Seventh Printing, 1981

Bugs Bunny smacked his lips. "Petunia," he said, "your plum preserves are just peachy!"

"Thank you, Bugs," said Petunia. "I hope the jam judges at the fair tomorrow agree with you."

Bugs was very busy. He was too lazy to enter the County Fair contests himself, but he loved giving orders to everyone else.

Bugs leaned out the kitchen window. "Porky, keep going!" he shouted. "You've got thirty-eight more seconds to do push-ups!"

"Poor Porky," sighed Petunia. "Do you *really* think he can swing that heavy hammer hard enough to ring the bell and win the prize?"

"Sure, if he wants to win badly enough," Bugs re-
plied. Setting his stopwatch, he looked out the window
again, then blew his whistle. "Take only a ten-second
break before you start jogging!" he reminded Porky.

Just then Little Cicero ran in, demanding, "Petunia,
I need another egg!"

"That's three eggs you've broken," scolded Petunia.

"I have to have eggs to practice with so I can win
the race tomorrow," Cicero explained.

"What race?" asked Bugs.

"The egg-and-spoon race at the fair," said Cicero,
reaching for the last egg in the carton.

"We'll hard-boil it first," suggested Bugs, putting the egg into a pan of water on the stove. "Then if it falls off your spoon, it'll just crack."

"But it's more fun when they break!" Cicero protested, watching his egg in the pan.

"Thank you, Bugs." Petunia laughed as Bugs bounded out the door, again blowing his whistle.

"It *can't* be ten seconds *yet!*" groaned Porky.

"It was ten seconds ten seconds ago," said Bugs. "On your feet—go! Be back in five and a half minutes. No stops! I'm timing you!"

As Porky jogged down the road, Bugs stretched out under a tree. He was just dozing off, when a familiar voice called over the fence, "What race are *you* trying to win?"

"What's up, doc?" called Bugs, looking over the fence at Elmer Fudd's garden. "Hey, your carrots are up! Would you like me to taste-test them?"

Reluctantly, Elmer handed him one. "I'm hoping
to sell the whole crop at the fair tomorrow."

"Yummy," said Bugs, reaching for another carrot.

"Only one to a taste-tester," said Elmer. "And don't
tell me you're practicing for a carrot-eating contest."

"Wish I'd thought of that." Bugs grinned. "I *never*
get enough carrots."

"The pie-eating contest is the only eating event at the fair," said Elmer.

"And Uncle Hogitall always wins." Bugs was remembering other fairs.

"Why don't *you* challenge him?" Elmer asked. "With your appetite, you might beat him."

Bugs thought it over. "Well, I haven't any jams to enter or crops to sell—"

"And you're too lazy to get into shape," Elmer added.

"But my appetite is *always* in shape," bragged Bugs. "Thanks for the suggestion, doc. When Porky gets back, tell him to chin himself eighteen times on the crab apple tree. I'm off to sign up for the pie-eating contest!"

But when Bugs got to the fairground, he found that the contest had been canceled.

"It's an outrage!" thundered Uncle Hogitall.

"You've won for eight years straight," snapped Judge Turtle. "This year, nobody has challenged you, so we're canceling the contest."

"Wait!" said Bugs. "I challenge Uncle Hogitall—
if I get to choose the kind of pie we eat."

"Don't you like blueberry pie?" asked the judge.

"I like carrot pie better," Bugs answered, smiling
hungrily.

"You want us to eat *carrot pies* for the contest?"
rumbled Uncle Hogitall.

"If it's okay with you, Judge Turtle, and the champ here," added Bugs, draping a friendly arm around Uncle Hogitall's shoulder.

After they agreed, Bugs signed up for the contest.

Next day, when the fair opened, an excited crowd gathered around a table stacked high with carrot pies. Would Bugs Bunny be able to outeat the all-time champion, Uncle Hogitall?

The champ arrived first. He sat down, tied a big napkin around his neck, and picked up a fork.

Then Bugs came, waved to the crowd, greeted Uncle Hogitall, tied on a napkin, and picked up a fork.

"Start eating!" shouted Judge Turtle.

"It's really unfair," murmured Bugs happily, chomping on his third pie. "I'm so *wild* about carrots!"

Then he noticed Uncle Hogitall smacking his lips over his *fourth* carrot pie.

"Better than blueberries!" commented the champ.

Meanwhile, Little Cicero easily won the egg-and-spoon race.

And Bugs and Uncle Hogitall kept eating.

Petunia proudly accepted a blue ribbon from the jam judges for her peachy plum preserves.

And Bugs and Uncle Hogitall ate on.

"*BONG!*" Porky swung the hammer, rang the bell, and won first prize for the highest score.

And Bugs and Uncle Hogitall each started on his *eighteenth* carrot pie.

"Must be something special about carrot pies," said
Judge Turtle. "Fourteen blueberry pies are the most
anybody's ever eaten before."

(And that was why Elmer Fudd sold *all* of his carrot
crop. His customers wanted to bake carrot pies!)

In the middle of his nineteenth pie, Uncle Hogitall
untied his napkin and laid down his fork with a sigh.
"I know when I'm licked," he said.

Judge Turtle raised Bugs Bunny's arm. "The winner and new champion pie-eater!" he announced.

The crowd roared, and Bugs hiccupped. For once in his life, he didn't want to see another carrot.

But his grateful friends didn't realize this.

Porky and Petunia were the first to visit Bugs after he got home. "It was your training that helped me win," said Porky.

"After you called my plum preserves 'peachy,' I added just a dab of peach," said Petunia. "*That's* what won me the blue ribbon."

Together, they handed Bugs a big box.

"I baked you a carrot cake," beamed Petunia.

"My favorite," said Bugs feebly. "Thank you."

When Elmer Fudd came calling, Bugs said, "I hear you sold *all* your carrots. Glad to hear it."

"Thanks to you, everyone wants carrot pies," said Elmer. "But I saved some, just for you—three bushels of the best ones!"

"Lovely," gulped Bugs. "Thanks, doc."

Later, when Bugs saw Little Cicero coming, he tried to hide behind the nearest tree. But he wasn't fast enough. The winner of the egg-and-spoon race handed him a brown paper bag.

Bugs peeked in. "Carrot candy!" he croaked. Then he lay down under the nearest tree to think about something very strange: *Too many carrots are too many carrots,* he realized, even for the greatest carrot-eater of them all!